ASTONISHING

Facts your friends won't believe!

Robert Bouffard

DEDICATION

To my family and friends whose interest, support, and encouragement made what sometimes felt overwhelming more like a pleasant pastime. And, especially, thank you to my wife, Karen. Your companionship has so enriched my life that I eagerly seek out the unusual so I can bring it home to you and share.

Preface

First, you read something astonishing – something tickles your curiosity. Then you're moved to do some hunting to enlarge your understanding, and that's a pleasure cruise in itself. You feel excited by your new-found knowledge, and share your discovery with friends. Now, a secondary reward takes place. Their response is another pleasure that extends itself beyond your own mind. Your work has excited other minds. Then, the miracle – you evolve into a story-teller. Everyone likes a good story. How you proceed will depend most on where your talents turn. Perhaps you write a book and include your precious gems. Maybe you're a teacher, and the new tidbit is just the delicacy needed to enliven student's minds. If you're asked to speak in public, you can use these little treasures to keep an audience's interest.

These truly astonishing facts are from my collection of oddities. Now they are part of your collection. Enjoy and savor.

My confession:

I was born with a curse, an unappeasable, fanatical curiosity. To me, new bits of knowledge only provoked a need for more information. I have lived with this curse as far back as I can remember. I assiduously record every newly discovered fact into my legion of journals. I use dollar-composition books by the carton. Perhaps it is just a zealous hobby, or maybe an uncommon addiction. But who was I hurting?

One night I received a call from my sister. She quietly told me that our father had passed away and that his commemorative service would be held in a week. My dad never much revealed to me about who he was inside. He had been a member of "The Greatest Generation" described by NBC journalist, Tom Brokaw, in his best-selling book of the same name. These were the rank and file of people who would come of age in the Great Depression. They persevered in the war against two of the most diabolical powers to ever confront our way of life in the US. And like many of that generation, my dad never talked about his hardships or war experiences.

As my sister and I went sadly through his things, I found his military medals and patches in a box shoved in a corner of his room. One of the patches revealed that our father had served in the First Air Force Combat Command. Eventually, from old family photos and some research, I learned that he was a 1st Lieutenant and trained new fighter pilots to fly the P 47 Thunderbolt in air-to-air combat. This helped me know him a little better.

Then I made a discovery that rocked my world! In the bottom drawer of his desk, far in the back, was an old wooden cigar box. I opened it and found it jam-packed with newspaper and magazine clippings. As I read them, I realized they were just a mass of interesting facts - hundreds of them!

My dad had suffered the same curse! I felt a new connection to my father that made me feel as if he was standing there by my side.

Most of my real education has come from my own personal reading. I began building a private library that eventually grew to over 4000 books. I would buy up boxes of books at yard sales and thrift stores. I would haunt used book stores and sit for hours savoring the smell of musty pages and discovering titles long out-of-print. Other than the one shelf of classics, my books were all non-fiction and covered more topics than any university curriculum.

Among my collection were books of quotations. These little treasures always intrigued me. Like poetry, they seemed like concentrated knowledge. The more you ponder them, the more your mind unfolds. Recently I came upon a quote by author Isaac Asimov that began to change my view of what my "curse" really represented. He said, "Man's greatest asset is the unsettled mind." What finally settled the matter for me came like an epiphany. It was a quote by astronomer and educator Maria Mitchell, "We have a hunger of the mind which asks for knowledge of all around us, and the more we gain, the more is our desire, the more we see, the more we are capable of seeing." I felt somehow absolved, even justified. A true conversion came over me. I was in good company with those of unquenchable curiosity.

My father's stockpile of factual gems had never been shared. What a shame. It wasn't long before another quote was to point an accusing finger at me. "Knowledge is power. Information is power. The secreting or hoarding of knowledge or information may be an act of tyranny camouflaged as humility", by Robin Morgan, in her best-selling book, <u>The Word of a</u>

<u>Woman.</u> I was "hoarding knowledge." I had imprisoned my discoveries in all those old journals and could, even should, share them with others. You, dear reader, now have the first product of my conversion.

I believe that in every obscure fact, there is a fragment of a much larger story. This collection of extraordinary story fragments is intended to excite your curiosity and enrich your imagination. Perhaps for you too, new ideas will grow in your mind and your world will become more tantalizing.

Robert Bouffard

"The best thing for being sad," replied Merlin, beginning to puff and blow, "is to learn something. That's the only thing that never fails. You may grow old and trembling in your anatomies, you may lie awake at night listening to the disorder of your veins, you may miss your only love, you may see the world about you devastated by evil lunatics, or know your honor trampled in the sewers of baser minds. There is only one thing for it then — to learn. Learn why the world wags and what wags it. That is the only thing which the mind can never exhaust, never alienate, never be tortured by, never fear or distrust, and never dream of regretting. Learning is the only thing for you. Look what a lot of things there are to learn."

- T.H. White

Grazing or resting cows tend to face north-south along the Earth's magnetic field lines. (Do they have a sixth sense? Think about that next time you order a hamburger. In what direction did you go after you ate it?) There is more to a cow than burgers – byproducts from these bovine creatures include explosives, chinaware, antifreeze, and tires. (It makes the saying "a bull in a china shop" a bit ironic, no?) What does a mobster have in common with a cow? Answer: a car explosion...tires, antifreeze, explosives – get it?

The 4th astronaut on the moon was raised in Roswell (hmmm...).

The Hollywood wanna-be movie mogul Howard Hughes' movie, *The Conqueror*, flopped due to casting John Wayne as the Asian Genghis Khan. Director Dick Powell had originally wanted Marlon Brando for the role. Wayne insisted he was just the man for the part. (Might as well cast Ringo Star as Christ for some bible movie, right?)

Currently, there are over 750,000 hunters this season in the state of Pennsylvania. If you were to organize those hunters into an army, Pennsylvania would have the 8th largest standing army in the world. That's more armed people than the entire Iranian Army, by almost 225,000. More than France and Germany combined. Toss in the combined hunters of, Wisconsin, Michigan, and West Virginia, which amount to over 1 and half million and it literally establishes the fact that the hunters of those four states alone would comprise the largest army in the world. And then add in the total number of hunters in the other 46 states. It's millions more. (The point: America will forever be safe from foreign invasion with that kind of home-grown firepower. Hunting - it's not just a way to fill the freezer. It's a matter of national security. What army of 2 million would want to face 50 million armed citizens?)

You've heard the term, "In the blink of an eye", but how much time is that? It is 100 milliseconds. (A second, divided into 1000 units, will be 1000 milliseconds.)

In the name of the daybreak
And the eyelids of morning
And the wayfaring moon
And the night when it departs,

I swear I will not dishonor
my soul with hatred
but offer myself humbly
as a guardian of nature,
as a healer of misery,
as a messenger of wonder,
as an architect of peace.

In the name of the sun and its mirrors
and the day that it embraces
and the cloud veils drawn over it
and the uttermost night
and the male and the female
and the plants bursting with seed
and the crowning seasons
of the firefly and the apple,

I will honor all life
- wherever and in whatever form
it may dwell – on earth my home,
and in the mansions of the stars.

- A hymn by Diane Ackerman, *Deep Play*

In Caesar's times, a common way to measure length was to use body parts like a hand or a foot. It was not exactly accurate because each person was different, but it was "handy" because you usually had these measuring instruments with you. A mile is was 5000 Roman feet.

Here's an interesting way to while away your time and have a little exercise at the same time. The average length of a person's step is two and a half feet. So, take 2112 steps and you've traveled about a mile. If you walk slow and take a second for each step, it'll take you a little over a half hour. This is much more exciting than watching paint dry.

There is a variety of orange called the Moro that, when fully ripe, has a rind the color of blood. And it has black flesh. (Perhaps they should have called it the Zombie orange).

"There are no seven wonders of the world in the eyes of a child. There are seven million."

- Walt Streightiff

The farthest you can see with the naked eye is 2.4 million light years away!

There is a book in the Library of Congress that is as small as the period at the end of this sentence. (Can someone hand me my reading glasses?) On the other side of the scale, there is a book there that stands 7 feet tall and is 5 feet across – with color pictures, yet!

The "just-an-innocent-teacher" you might remember reading about in the Scopes Monkey Trial of 1925, was charged and found guilty of teaching evolution to his class. But it was actually part of a staged action and trial! The teacher, John T. Scopes, purposely incriminated himself at the behest of the American Civil Liberties Union, which financed the whole thing. Worse yet, he wasn't even the regular teacher. He was serving as a substitute that day. Later, John Butler, Tennessee State Representative, who initiated the law against teaching evolution, admitted that he knew nothing about evolution.

In Chapter Four of Alice's Adventures in Wonderland, Alice comes upon a hookah-smoking caterpillar sitting on a mushroom. Now remember, the author Charles Dodson, (pen-name Lewis Carroll), was a mathematician, not a botanist or a bug man. Yet he has this caterpillar smoking a hookah and the original book's illustration even has etchings of nearby tobacco plants. The book was published almost 150 years ago, and yet it wasn't until 2015 that scientists discovered that the hornworm caterpillar, which looks surprisingly similar to the Wonderland illustration, wards off predators by venting foul-smelling nicotine acquired by chomping on tobacco leaves.

In several modern languages, the orange is known as "Chinese apple", while in English, Chinese apple usually refers to a pomegranate.

Solivagant – (adj.) wandering alone

The Burro banana has squared sides and a lemon flavor when ripe. Aptly named because their stubby stature is reminiscent to that of a donkey or burro. While they have a variety of culinary uses, they have also been used to stimulate hemoglobin in cases of anemia.

There seems to be a field full of ways to break in a new baseball glove. Most are hotly debated as being the best and many border on just plain weird. Some say to bake it in an oven until it begins to smell like steak. Others say you have to beat it into submission with a baseball bat or run over it a few times with your car. But conservative experts say to wet down a towel in hot tap water, put a hardball deep into the pocket of the glove, then wrap the towel tightly around the glove, tie it with an old athletic sock and let it hang out to dry a few days.

Both Nathan Hale's famous, "I regret that I have but one life to lose for my country" and Patrick Henry's demand, "Give me Liberty or give me death", were borrowed from a play popular at that time. In fact, the play, *Cato*, by the 18th century playwright Joseph Addison, was so honored and inspirational, General Washington had it performed for his ragged troops at Valley Forge.

> "I went to the woods because I wished to live deliberately, to front only the essential facts of life, and see if I could not learn what it had to teach, and not, when I came to die, discover that I had not lived."
>
> - Henry David Thoreau

Eugene O'Neil penned a play that lasted 5 hours.

90% of the few remaining lion populations in Botswana, South Africa and Tanzania infected with FIV which is simialr to our HIV.

Leather holster manufacturers recommend that you unholster and then reholster your firearm to "break in" the new holster – only you do this 150 times! Of course, don't wait until the day before the expected gunfight to do this. Your hand may be partially paralyzed for awhile.

The Mohawk Indians called their neighboring tribe, the "Adirondacks", which translates to "tree eaters". This is due to their practice of using the cambium layer of tree bark to make a sort of bread, accordingly called "bark bread". The moist, soft, white inner bark just beneath the outer bark is edible. Dried and ground into a powder, it can be used as a type of flour and made into bread high in vitamins A and C. It can also be eaten raw or used as a thickener in soups and stews.

In proportion to weight, your jaw muscles are the strongest in your body – and each one, the right or left muscle can impart 900 pounds of force per square inch of jaw. If your teeth could withstand the pressure, you'd be able to chew concrete and cinder block. You could even puncture a truck tire.

Koalas and primates are the only animals with unique fingerprints.

If you've ever gone back through a photo album and found yourself asking "where in the world was that picture taken?" then a geotag is the answer to your prayers. This portmanteau refers to the act of imbedding intricate geographical information (usually latitude and longitude) into a digital media file. Many GPS-equipped cameras allow you to geotag your photos and videos, so that even the weariest travelers will always remember where they were when they saw what they saw.

"Or could I feel the starlight? Every minute on a square mile of this land -on the steers and the orchard, the meadow, and creek – one ten thousandth of an ounce of starlight spatters to the earth. What percentage of an ounce did that make on my eyes and cheeks and arms, tapping and nudging as particles, pulsing and stroking as waves?"

– Annie Dillard

Gravity will accelerate any object at a rate of *32 feet per second per second*. But what do we do with that number? What it means is that if we fall for one *second* we'll reach a speed of *32 feet per second*. After two *seconds* we reach 64 *feet per second*, etc.

The tallest mountain is in the US. It's Mauna Kea in Hawaii - 6 miles high, (but 3 miles of the mountain is under water). If you begin your measurement from the center of Earth to the highest point on the surface, Mount Everest is only the fifth furthest point. The tallest mountain yet discovered is Olympus Mons – 15 miles high! (But you need a space suite to climb it. The mighty volcano is on Mars).

The next time you're on the third floor of a building, look out a window and imagine a snake that, if it was standing on its tail, would be staring into your eyes – it's the reticulated python, the longest snake in the world. At thirty feet, it is big enough to swallow and digest wild pigs, antelope, monkeys, and even humans. (Back slowly away from the window).

As scary as tarantulas are, here is something just recently learned that adds to the nightmare. They can shoot sticky silk from their feet to keep from slipping off a vertical surface. (Many pet stores sell tarantulas but should warn new owners to cover their enclosures while Spiderman movies are on.)

There are over 600 different types of oranges.

"Facts are to the mind what food is to the body"

- Edmund Burke

People who study spiders are called arachnologists. In Greek mythology, Arachne was a mortal woman who made the mistake of challenging a goddess, Athena, saying she was a better weaver. Arachne lost the weaving contest and was so insulting to the goddess that her second place art work was torn to shreds. Anguished, Arachne hung herself. (Talk about a poor loser!) Athena had mercy on her, of a sort. She restored Arachne back to life - as a spider!

We owe pigs a higher honor than to just turn them into bacon. After all, the best insulin for diabetics comes from pigs. Heart valves from pigs are successfully transplanted into humans. John Wayne lived several more years because of a pig heart transplant.

Columbus brought the first orange seeds to Europe.

A Japanese collector paid almost a million dollars for a dusty malfunctioning Hasselbad camera that was used by astronauts on the moon. Did they clean it up before proceeding – no! The dust on it made it the more valuable because it was moon dust. Its malfunction was the reason it was returned to earth. NASA needed the film intact. Other cameras and equipment were routinely left behind on the moon to make room for rock and mineral samples being brought back. But, talk about litterbugs! Astronauts really have left a lot of "trash" back on the moon: things like golf balls, 12 pairs of boots, various tools, blankets, hygiene kits, backpacks, empty cartons of space food, memorial tributes, and even 96 bags of excreta. (Wonder what price those bags would fetch?)

Orange peel is used by gardeners as a slug repellent.

In Germany, the "shhh" sound literally means hurry up.

"It is important to realize that what one neuron tells another neuron is simply how much it is excited."

- Francis Crick, *The Astonishing Hypothesis*

A lion can hear its prey from a mile away. The roar of a fully grown lion can be heard from five miles away.

Experts estimate that more than 20,000 species go extinct each year – that's more than 50 each day. The rate of extinction is getting higher each year - because of us. They even have a name for this type of extinction. It's called "background extinction", as opposed to natural extinction which would take place without our pushing it. We are currently using 25% more of our natural resources per year than the planet can replenish.

Attempts to memorize the value of π with increasing precision have led to records of over 70,000 digits.

We all have heard of a landfill. But an oceanfill? Covering over a square mile of ocean floor, there is an artificial reef just off the coast of Slaughter Beach, Delaware, made up of 1.292 old New York Redbird subway cars, 86 decommissioned military tanks, armored personal carriers, 3,000 tons of weighted truck tires and even eight tugboats. They call it Red Reef because of the bold red colors of the subway cars. The reef has so successfully promoted marine life (some estimates put the increase at 400 times the original amount) that it has become a popular fishing and scuba diving location, and has other states begging for the next subway cars for their "oceanfill."

"Carry the spirit of a child. Just keep getting excited about things and see the world as massive and unending inspiration, color and dreams. Spread those sparks around so that everyone is on fire too because wonder is a contagious burning thing that fuels adulthood like the slingshot of an arrow - the rush it brings."

- Victoria Erickson

There is a variety of orange called Pineapple.

In a special study conducted in 1980, scientists were stunned by the unexpected diversity of beetles within the limited habitat of just 19 trees grouped together in a Panamanian jungle – eighty percent of the beetles were previously unknown to science. It is distressing that we know more about the number of stars in our galaxy than the number of species here on earth.

In 1919, a ship called Ethie crashed into rocks, stranding 93 sailors amidst stormy seas. After one of the sailors was swept out to sea, the crew turned to Tang. With a rope in his mouth, the dog leaped into the water. When he reached land, onlookers were amazed to discover that his jaw was still fastened to the rope. All 92 of the remaining sailors were pulled to safety due to Tang's ceaseless bravery.

The Eiffel Tower was originally intended to be just a temporary structure for the World Fair in Paris. When the creator, Gustave Eiffel, discovered that the people of Paris planned to designate it as a permanent landmark, even he confessed "France will be the only country in the world to have a 300 meter flagpole".

Kefir is a fermented drink enjoyed by the people of China. It is made from the milk of the horse. It is said that the process of milking the horse, (being especially careful to pick a mare, not a stallion), takes considerable skill.

We've all heard strange stories of the Bermuda Triangle, or the Devil's Triangle, as some may call it. But the exact region has never been precisely defined. The US Navy denies it even exists and its name is not recognized by the US Board on Geographic Names, (try finding it on any legitimate map). The Triangle got its name in popular culture after its most infamous incident. On December 5, 1945, a squadron of five Navy torpedo bombers took off from Naval Air Station, Ft. Lauderdale, Florida, on a standard training flight. Later radio transmissions indicated they had somehow gotten lost and all 14 airmen were never heard from again. Even a huge PBM Mariner patrol bomber flying boat with a 13-man crew trying to find the torpedo bombers ended in oblivion. Subsequent searches by other planes and ships turned up nothing. To this day, no signs of the planes have been found. It was this incident that created "The Bermuda Triangle".

The banana tree is actually an herb. A bunch of bananas is called a "hand", which it resembles.

"Seize the moment of excited curiosity."

- William Wirt

The smallest known dinosaur was 4 inches tall.

The Nigerian Putty-nosed monkey has two alarm calls – one for the jungle leopard, "pyow" and one for the eagle, "hack" – both common predators that pose a danger to the monkeys. But researchers have recently discovered another distinct alarm call that is a combination of the two, as in the sequence "pyow pyow hack hack hack hack," which means, "Let's get out of here," used to summon the younger monkeys, ". (Find a photo of this simian and you'll find it looks like a painter slapped a gob of white putty on its nose – so alluring, yes?

If you tickle a rat, it quickly emits a high-pitched giggle.

Australia, land of kangaroos, has nearly half a million wild camels running around. Were it not for hunters it would be in the millions. Australia, land of camels?

You often see the portrait of Benjamin Franklin flying his kite as a very old man with his gray hair awry and flowing in the storm's breeze, his hand reaching out to the key connected to the kite string. Well, there's considerable artistic license at play here. At the time of this experiment, Franklin was a robust 46 year old man and was accompanied by his illegitimate son William, who was twenty three years old. They were alone because Franklin was unsure of the outcome and didn't want to expose himself to any public ridicule. He was lucky he didn't electrocute the both of them. Had lightning actually struck the kite, as some stories tells us, it would most probably have killed them both. Franklin had made certain they both were on dry ground during the experiment and that the portion of kite string they were holding was not wet. (Don't try this at home. Several other would-be scientists who tried to replicate this experiment died of electrocution in the process.)

The lion has the largest mouth in the animal kingdom, a foot wide when fully grown.

"Gardeners may create order briefly out of chaos, but nature always gets the last word, and what it says is usually untidy by human standards. But I find all states of nature beautiful, and because I want to delight in my garden, not rule it, I just accept my yen to tame the chaos on one day and let the Japanese beetles run riot on the next."

- Diane Ackerman

Leafcutter ants cut leaves with jaws that vibrate 1000 times per second. (Compare that to a hummingbird's wing beat at a mere 50 times a second.) The ants bury the masticated leaf remnants in an underground garden where they farm a fungus that is their main food source.

The chicken is considered to be the closest generic species to the T. Rex dinosaur.

Patients with aphasia can no longer speak, read or write. Yet they are better lie detectors than the modern polygraph machines. The language disorder is usually caused by stroke or head injury. Because they are not misguided by the meaning of words coming out of the mouth of someone talking, they are exquisitely sensitive to all the nonverbal signs and subtle nuances of expression. One doctor, a neurologist working with aphasic patients at a hospital, heard them all laughing hysterically in the recreation room. When he went to investigate this strange outbreak, he discovered they were all watching a televised speech by the reigning president.

At the time Rosa Parks refused to move from her seat in a white section of a segregated bus in Alabama, she had already spent the past ten years as the only female in the local chapter of the National Association for the Advancement of Colored People. So, the story of the weary seamstress, too tired to get up and move to back of the bus, was, you might say, poetic license.

"If you ask one question, it will lead you to another, and another. It's like peeling an onion."

- Lemony Snicket

Currently, there is more than 2.2 billion square feet of storage space in the US provided by a billion dollar storage facility industry. That's enough space for every US citizen, man, woman and child, to stand in shoulder-to-shoulder with a roof over their heads. It seems we use this vast space to store old stuff so we surround ourselves with new stuff.

The navel orange is the result of an orange with a conjoined twin growing within the same primary peel.

Remember when your mother would scold you for leaving food on your dinner plate? She says, "Eat your vegetables. Do you know how many children are starving in China?" I'd always say (in my mind), "Then why don't we just send these leftovers to China?" As I got older, I read the real statistics on world hunger and discovered, to my horror, that an estimated 22,000 children die each <u>day</u> due to poverty. Even after starving children have been rescued, many do not survive. Their digestive systems have shut down and can no longer process the incoming nutrients in time to save them from starvation. (So I've learned to say a blessing before meals, and to nurture a sincere gratitude for each bite.)

The Golden gate bridge is made up of enough steel cables to extend around the equator three times.

Farmers sometimes give their pigs Coca Cola to dissolve gastrointestinal bezoars, large wads of indigestible plant material, such as fibers, skins and seeds. When the farmer observes his pig is not putting on weight, eating less and not passing gas at all – time for a Coke!

Sweat is not made up of toxins from your body, and the belief that sweat can cleanse the body is a myth. Toxins such as mercury, alcohol and most drugs are eliminated by your liver, intestines or kidneys. Inducing perspiration through the use of a "purification" sweat lodge, or heavy exercise, can cause your kidneys to save water and actually hang on to any toxins that may be circulating in your system.

When you cough, air moves through your windpipe faster than the speed of sound – over a thousand feet per second!

> "The mind once enlightened cannot again become dark."
>
> - Thomas Paine

Dalmatians are born pure white. Their spots grow in later. They are prone to deafness. The more white that is in their coat, the more likely they'll be deaf, psychotic, a real airhead and have torturous urinary problems. (Get a Dalmatian that is mostly white with beautiful blue eyes, and you'll get a dog that is deaf to your commands, will never understand what you want even if it heard you, will likely bite the neighborhood children, and will whine when it's using a fire hydrant. How special!)

Arachnologists, (spider specialists), estimate that there are now more than 40,000 species of spiders. Each spider spins more than one type of silk. Bioprospectors, people who search for new materials among natural sources, believe spider's silk is the toughest biological material in the world. They estimate that there are as many as 200,000 different kinds of spider silk. Of all the types of silk, the one they found strung by the Bark Spider across 80 feet of a river in Madagascar is 10 times tougher than Kevlar, the bullet-proof stuff police and military wear. They don't know how it's made, nor do they know why it's so strong – to catch what? (Anybody for a nice romantic canoe ride down the river to watch the Madagascar sunset...anybody?)

We've found beneficial uses of nearly 70,000 plant species alone. When you consider that we have discovered less than 2 million species so far, and experts estimate there are probably as many as 20 million more we have not even heard of yet, it boggles the imagination as to how many benefits nature would have provided us if we hadn't made them disappear first.

Cell phones cause hearing loss. According to a study conducted by the American Academy of Otolaryngology, cell phone use exceeding 60 minutes per day could result in lasting damage such as high frequency hearing loss. Those with high frequency hearing loss cannot hear sounds ranging from 2,000 to 8,000 Hertz, which can affect the ability to understand speech and discern consonants. It's not the volume but the electromagnetic waves emitted by the phone that cause damage.

On the grounds of a monastery in Bahia, Brazil, sits the original orange tree that bore the mutation we now know as the navel orange. Since the orange is seedless, (sterile), it cannot propagate the usual way and must be grafted onto other varieties of citrus trees. So all navel oranges can be considered coming from that one single 200 year-old parent tree.

A human fetus acquires distinct fingerprints at the age of three months.

Some of the dinosaur sounds in the movie "Jurassic Park" came from recordings of a tortoise having sex.

> "It is, in fact, nothing short of a miracle that the modern methods of instruction have not yet entirely strangled the holy curiosity of inquiry; for this delicate little plant, aside from stimulation, stands mainly in need of freedom. Without this it goes to wrack and ruin without fail."
>
> - Albert Einstein

According to researchers, there can be as many as 1.2 million bacteria on a single toothbrush.

The Rapunzel syndrome is a rare intestinal condition in humans resulting from eating hair. The syndrome is named after the long-haired girl in the fairy tale by the Brothers Grimm, *"Rapunzel, Rapunzel, let down your hair, so that I may climb thy golden stair."* Since hair is indigestible, it can accumulate in the stomach and form a large hair ball called a trichobezoar. In extreme cases the "tail" of the hair ball can extend into the intestines and block the passageway. This can be fatal if misdiagnosed. (And that is no fairy tale!)

By reducing moisture loss, petroleum jelly can prevent chapped lips, and soften nail cuticles. More than 140 years ago, a young chemist, Robert Cheesbrough, began to study "rod wax", a byproduct of oil drilling, for its purported healing properties. (Oil workers were using it to heal wounded or burnt skin). He eventually refined the substance and patented it as "Wonder Jelly." He later decided to rebrand the product as Vaseline®, a combination of the German word for water, wasser, and the Greek word for oil, oleon.

The Bergamot orange peel is worth more than what is inside. Grown mainly in Italy, the peel is what gives Earl Grey tea its distinct flavor and aroma.

Like fingerprints, every individual has a unique tongue print that can be used for identification. ("Yes, Mr. President. In order to initiate a nuclear strike, it will require two high-ranking officers to simultaneously lick the trigger buttons.")

It takes 10,600 jasmine flowers and 28 dozen May roses to make a single ounce of the "costliest perfume in the world." Joy, a light floral perfume, was created by French perfumer Jean Patou in 1930 to lift the spirits of his clientele during the Great Depression. Today, a single ounce of this eau de toilette runs around $600. The sticky resin from the Mediterranean shrub labdanum or brown-eyed rock rose used in the formulation has an odor that is very rich, complex and tenacious. The fragrant oil contained from this resin was historically used as religious incense and had medicinal uses as well. The resin coats the leaves of the rose plant and in ancient times goats were herded through the shrubs and then the resin combed from their coats and beards. Some historians believe that the false beards worn by the Egyptian pharaohs symbolize the beard of the goats used for this purpose.

A lion's tongue can peel away the prey's skin just by licking.

"I would rather entertain and hope that people learned something than educate people and hope they were entertained"

- Walt Disney

John Wayne died of cancer, which many medical experts believe he contracted by inhaling radioactive dust from a movie set of "The Conqueror" in Utah, downwind from where the military had detonated 11 atomic bombs just two years before the filming. This was a disastrous movie by Howard Hughes. (Can't imagine John Wayne as the Asian Genghis Khan?) The cast and crew survived the 120 degree heat, a flash flood, and a panther attack, but because of the radioactive dust, 91 finally contracted cancer. Hughes even had 60 tons of "hot" dirt carted back to a set in Hollywood to finish up production shots there. (Wonder whose garden that dirt's in now?) Hughes was so guilty about the whole affair that he would watch that movie night after night during his last paranoid years.

Turkeys can reproduce without having sex. It's called parthenogenesis. The turkey was wrongly named after its believed country of origin. The bird has many vocalizations: "gobbles", "clucks", "putts", "purrs", "yelps", "cutts", "whines", "cackles", and "kee-kees".

All FDA–approved pharmaceutical companies in the US have barred the sale of their drugs to corrections agencies. European drug companies have banned the export of these drugs as well. This means that states that use lethal injection for executions must now go underground to get hold of the medicines. States that have done this have been challenged in court for their covert activities. Experiments with new drugs are under way, but have resulted in botched executions. Some inmates have suffered excruciating pain due to a violent reaction to the drugs. (Yeah, sorry governor, but I'm allergic to lethal injections).

It wasn't until 2005, that the US abolished the act of putting to death children under the age of 18.

The kick of an ostrich can kill a lion.

"The mockingbird took a single step into the air and dropped. His wings were still folded against his sides as though he were singing from a limb and not falling, accelerating thirty-two feet per second per second, through empty air. Just a breath before he would have been dashed to the ground, he unfurled his wings with exact, deliberate care, revealing the broad bars of white, spread his elegant, white-banded tail, and so floated onto the grass. I had just rounded a corner when his insouciant step caught my eye; there was no one else in sight. The fact of his free fall was like the old philosophical conundrum about the tree that falls in the forest. The answer must be, I think, that beauty and grace are performed whether or not we will or sense them. The least we can do is try to be there."

- Annie Dillard

The fax machine was invented 33 years before the telephone.

One of the most outstanding artists of his genre was Victor Lustig, a con artist, "The man who sold the Eiffel Tower. Twice." In 1925, there were rumors that Paris officials were discussing the removal of the Eiffel Tower because the cost of the upkeep was taxing the city's budget. Victor, using fake government stationary and identification papers invited six scrap metal dealers to a secret meeting and told them that because of the sensitive nature of the matter their bids would be kept secret. Victor had done his home work and took Andre Poisson aside and told him he would accept a bribe to take his bid. Andre was a vain, insecure businessman and wanted the honor enough to not only pay the bribe but also provide the full bid amount in advance. Victor took off to Vienna with a suitcase full of money. When Poisson finally discovered that he had been duped, he was too embarrassed to go to the police and Victor was never prosecuted for the deception –until the second time he tried the same thing on six other scrap metal dealers not so naïve a month later. He failed to get the money but did manage to escape arrest. Later, Victor was to entice even Al Capone in a clever swindle. He convinced "Scarface" to invest $50,000 with him on a stock-market "sure deal". Victor just put the money in a safe deposit box and two months later returned the money to Al saying the deal had gone awry. Capone was so impressed with this man's "integrity", he rewarded him $1000 – which was what Victor was betting on all the time. Ironically, both men would end up in Alcatraz at the same time – Capone, eight years for tax evasion, and Lustig, twenty years for counterfeiting.

Besides Mona Lisa, Gold Finger, Ice Cream and Blue Java, there are more than 1000 types of bananas.

A school in Colorado had to be evacuated with a hazmat crew on site washing down contaminated students and teachers and some of the students even needing hospitalization – the cause – the toxic irritant was just six habanera chili peppers found among the wood chips on the playground. Just stepping on them had sent up a minuscule spray that caused the whole scene. Scientific tests have shown pepper spray, which uses Capsaicin as their main ingredient, is more severe than tear gas.

Some stomach cancer patients have to live without a stomach. In this case, your doctor will connect your esophagus to your small intestine. You can live this way, but your body may not be able to absorb some vitamins.

"The larger the island of knowledge, the longer the shoreline of wonder."

- Ralph W. Sockman

Burning Feet syndrome, also known as Grierson-Gopalan syndrome, is a medical condition that causes severe burning and aching of the feet. (This reminds me of the Anthony Robbins' team-building firewalking exercise. Only these people actually walked on a bed of hot coals without any burns.)

In 1908, a Japanese scientist discovered a new taste. Beyond the basic sweet, sour, salty and bitter, he called this new taste, umami (Japanese for delicious). Umami is described as brothy or meaty. Umami has a mild but lasting aftertaste associated with salivation and a sensation of furriness on the tongue, stimulating the throat, the roof and the back of the mouth. Without even knowing its chemical source, the French chef Auguste Escoffier became famous for his use of this flavor in his secret recipes. Many humans' first encounter with umami components is breast milk. It contains roughly the same amount of umami as meat broths.

"Anyone who stops learning is old, whether at twenty or eighty. Anyone who keeps learning stays young."

- Henry Ford

The original Bill of Rights started out as twelve proposed amendments to the American Constitution. But when you see the "official" Bill of Rights, (the one on display under bullet-proof glass at Wash DC), there are only ten. One of the missing two was ratified only after a whopping 203 years later. It is now the Twenty-seventh Amendment. (No, I'm not going to spoil the fun – look it up yourself). If it's been awhile since you've familiarized yourself with our country's Constitution, then you're not alone. Recent surveys show that the majority of Americans are ignorant of even when the Constitution was signed – they confuse it with the 1776 signing of the Declaration of Independence. While both were signed in the same Hall in Philadelphia the Constitution was signed eleven years later.

Auguste Escoffier, one of the world's most famous French chefs, invented over 10,000 recipes. He also introduced the idea of the ala carte menu. Head chef to many famous restaurants of his time, his popularity changed the style of formal dining. Prior to his time, restaurants were primarily an all-men's affair. It was unseemly to have a woman eat in public. The age of French cooking under the mastering of Escoffier changed all that.

Although the word 'ketchup' by itself usually refers to tomato ketchup, it may also be used to describe sauces from other vegetables or fruits, such as banana ketchup, and the always popular asparagus (yuk!) ketchup.

> "Curiosity is only vanity. Most frequently we wish not to know, but to talk. We would not take a sea voyage for the sole pleasure of seeing without hope of ever telling."
>
> - Blaise Pascal

Studies have shown that searing a piece of meat, such as a steak, to keep the juices in, actually dries the steak out. It is the steak's juices your hear sizzling as they evaporate from the pan. But your mind tricks you into thinking the seared steak is juicier than the slow cooked one due to expectations – your increased saliva makes it seem juicier. Also the crisp outer crust of the seared meat contrasted with the juicer inner portion gives the illusion of a juicier steak.

It's possible for your body to survive without a surprisingly large fraction of its internal organs. Even if you lose your stomach, your spleen, 75% of your liver, 80% of your intestines, one kidney, one lung, and virtually every organ from your pelvic and groin area, you wouldn't be very healthy, but you would live.

The American lobster can zip through the water at a rate of up to 25 feet a second.

In North Korea they have a death penalty for watching South Korean movies.

"Our sense of self thrives in those minute spaces, convergence zones where puzzles become pictures and concepts. We haunt the synapses, tiny intersections throughout the brain where traffic stalls, collides, or drives across. The space between two neurons, called a synaptic junction, provides a narrow where they meet to send and receive news. It is a small liquid space, as in the air between two whispering lovers, yet so much life happens there. Each junction is a bazaar full of commerce, intrigue, and possibility. In the brain, everything depends on almost nothing, a lively space, the vital channel between neurons."

– Diane Ackerman, *An Alchemy of Mind*

During your lifetime, you will produce enough saliva to fill two swimming pools. Actually, Saliva is more than just drool. If your saliva cannot dissolve something, you cannot taste it.

Queen ants sleep longer than worker ants – a queen's naps add up to over 9 hours per day. By contrast, workers are forced to cope by taking hundreds of short power naps that add up to only half that. Queen ants fall into relatively long, deep sleeps and there is even an indication that they dream. This division of rest may help explain why queens live for years, while worker ants typically only live for months. It also ensures that enough worker ants are awake at any one time to protect the nest and that jobs never go unattended. On average, a single worker ant takes 250 naps each day, with each one lasting just over a minute. This means that 80 per cent of the workforce is awake and active at any one time. There is always a worker available when the need arises. When work is slow, workers sleep more.

"The cure for boredom is curiosity. There is no cure for curiosity".

- Dorothy Parker

The three things pregnant women dream most of during their first trimester are frogs, worms and potted plants. Scientists have no idea why this is so, but attribute the odd dreams to the growing imbalance of hormones in the body during pregnancy.

Since the 1960s, thanks to widespread use of polio vaccines, polio has been eliminated from most of the world, and it is now endemic only in several countries of Africa and South Asia. Approximately 1,000–2,000 children are still paralyzed by polio each year, most of them in India.

More video content is created on You Tube in a 60 day period than the three major U.S. television networks created in the last 80 years.

The pointed hoods of the KKK are called capuchins, named after an order of early Christian monks. The monks adopted the robes and hoods as a sign of their chosen hermit life, modeled after the life of Saint Francis of Assisi. The little monkeys seen with a beggar's cup at the feet of the organ grinders of yore are Capuchin monkeys. The color of their fur surrounding their faces makes them appear to be wearing hoods.

"It is our task to imprint this temporary, perishable earth into ourselves so deeply, so painfully and passionately, that its essence can arise again…We are the bees of the invisible…[Our work is] the continual conversation of the beloved visible and tangible world into the invisible vibrations and agitation of our own nature."

- Rainer Maria Rilke

Schizophrenia, although the Greek means "split -mind", does not refer to a split personality, (multiple personality disorder), but to a split with reality, such as hallucinations, paranoia, inability to experience pleasure, etc. In one uncommon subtype of this, the person may be mute and remain motionless in bizarre postures for long periods of time. Up to 50% have no insight that they have this condition. Parenting style has been shown to have no major effect, although living in an urban environment during childhood increases risk by a factor of two. While some studies have shown that cannabis can be a contributory factor in schizophrenia, a significant proportion of schizophrenics use the drug to sufficiently deal with their condition.

The Library of Congress is the nation's oldest federal cultural institution and serves as the research arm of Congress. It is also the largest library in the world. The Law Library has grown over the years to become the world's largest law library, with a collection of over three million volumes spanning the ages and covering virtually every jurisdiction in the world.

> "Knowledge is love and light and wisdom".
>
> - Helen Keller

That delicious white sugar icing on top of cheap Danish, (the Danes call it "Viennese bread"), comes from glops of titanium dioxide, the same substance found in white latex paint.

Applying Vitamin C to the skin topically is up to 20 times more effective than taking it orally.

Bats range in size from the giant flying foxes, with wingspans up to 5 feet, to the itty-bitty bumblebee bat, with only a 6-inch wingspan.

A standard microwave will pummel a food with electromagnetic rays at approx 147 billion times per minute.

The Cure for Insomnia, directed by John Henry Timmis IV, is the longest film by running time in the world. It is 87 hours long, (3 days and 15 hours). The film has no plot, instead consisting of artist L. D. Groban reading his 4,080-page poem "A Cure for Insomnia", spliced with occasional clips from "Heavy Metal Music" and pornographic videos. It was first played in its entirety at the Art Institute of Chicago from January 31 to February 3, 1987, in one continuous showing. It has not been released on DVD or other home video formats. It would have filled 22 disks. (Can't wait for it).

Zimbabwe, a country in South Africa, has 16 official languages.

Kim Jong- Il, late leader of North Korea, (and father to the current supreme leader Kim Jong-un), was so fussy about his food that he hired a member of his staff to inspect his rice, insisting that every grain be the same size. Although he was only 5'3" tall, he ordered that all short or disabled people be deported from the capital, Pyongyang.

"It is easier to believe a lie that one has heard a thousand times than to believe a fact that no one has heard before".

- Anon

Albert Einstein was born on Pi Day (3/14/1879). (pi - π , the ratio of a circle's circumference to its diameter)

On May 28, 1987, a West German pilot named Mathias Rust successfully landed his light aircraft at St. Basil, next to Red Square, causing a major scandal in the Soviet Air Defense Forces. This would be the equivalent to landing a private plane on the White House lawn without being challenged.

Alessandro Volta, physicist, chemist and a pioneer of electrical science, discovered "contact electricity" resulting from contact between different metals. He first described electric current by putting a cooper coin on one side of his tongue and a zinc coin on the other and then letting the two just barely touch each other - he called the tingling sensation a current because it seemed to be like a stream into a river.

Russia used to own Alaska, after colonizing it in 1733, but sold to US in 1867 - 13 years before gold was discovered there.

Every child has written their names on the beach at some point. But whereas most people's "sandwriting" is washed away, one super-rich Arab sheikh has ensured that his doodles will last a little longer. Hamad Bin Hamdan Al Nahyan, 63, has scrawled his name in sand on an island he owns with letters so big they can be seen from space. The word 'HAMAD' is a staggering two miles long from the "H" to the "D". It would take you half an hour just to walk from the bottom of the letter "H" to the top. And rather than allow the writing to be washed away by the ocean, the letters actually form waterways that absorb the encroaching tide. The ruler's name is even visible on Google's map service.

"Live as if you were to die tomorrow. Learn as if you were to live forever."

- Mahatma Gandhi

There are thousands of varieties of peppers, ranging in size and hotness, but the black table pepper we use in salt and pepper shakers isn't even in the same family. It is a fruit like a peach and cherry. The fruit seeds from these red berries are peppercorns, and the ground pepper derived from them may be described simply as pepper, or more precisely as black pepper (cooked and dried unripe fruit), green pepper (dried unripe fruit) and white pepper (ripe fruit seeds).

Alexander Lukashenko, President of Belarus. Neighbor to Poland, is a hockey fanatic and likes to train with the National team – his body guards won't allow any blocking. (Reminds me of the comedy movie where the dictator runs track and trips his opponents, shoots the lead runner and shoots the referee to win the race).

Eskimos put seagulls in bottles of water and let them ferment in the sun for legitimate seagull wine.

In Mauritania, Africa, women are fattened for marriage because fat equals beauty there.

"In all things of nature there is something of the marvelous."

-Aristotle

Studies have shown that men get more of an endorphin rush from eating the capsaicin in curry than from kissing their partner. Curry is a primary ingredient in Indian cooking.

60% of the world population cannot digest milk.

The Russian president Medvedev signed a bill that, for the first time, officially classified beer as alcoholic. Before, anything with less than 10% alcohol was a foodstuff. There are 7 million alcoholics in Russia. Almost half of all deaths of working age men in Russia are from alcohol consumption. The sale of men's aftershave had to be banned before lunchtime in Moscow because so many alcoholics were drinking the stuff.

The famous stage actress of the early 1900's, Lillie Langtry, was the first female celebrity to endorse a commercial product. It was her lily-white skin that attracted the English Pear Soap Company. The fee they paid her was allied to her weight, which meant, she was paid literally "pound for pound".

Biologists have discovered that cockroaches can change course as many as 25 times in one second.

> "I find that a great part of the information I have was acquired by looking up something and finding something else on the way."
>
> — Franklin P. Adams

The castor bean plant is used extensively as a decorative plant in parks and other public areas. But, just chewing two castor beans can kill you. The bean contains the chemical ricin - 200 times more toxic than cyanide. Castor bean oil, when broken down in a chemical process, produces aromatic esters which are used to create artificial fruit flavors--including jasmine, apricot, peach, plum, rose, banana and lemon. Ironically, raw castor oil itself is renowned for its bad stench. Castor bean oil is also a primary ingredient required for the manufacture of nylon; each ton of nylon produced requires roughly 3 tons of castor bean oil. (Warning – do not chew pantyhose, right?)

Today you'll find a remarkable light bulb burning bright at a fire station in Livermore, California. It hasn't been turned off since 1901, shining around the clock (save for a few brief interruptions) for nearly one million hours now. The Guinness Book of World Records, Ripley's Believe It Or Not and General Electric agree the four-watt, carbon filament bulb is the longest-burning in history.

Cassava roots and leaves are poisonous – just 40 mg of pure cassava cyanogenic glucoside is enough to kill a cow. We are most familiar with cassava in the form of tapioca.

The distance that food is transported has escalated dramatically. It has been estimated that the typical contents of an American shopping cart for the family have travelled over 95,000 miles – nearly four times around the world. The beans might come from Kenya or Peru, apples from New Zealand or South Africa, asparagus from Egypt, and baby corn from Thailand.

At one time McDonald's fries were dipped in sugar before being fried in vegetable oil that had beef flavoring added to it.

There are three different species of blood-drinking vampire bats.

"...that rare mental disease that allows for dissociated facts to become a new truth or discovery."

- Friedrich Nietzsche

The Bergamot orange is so bitter it can't be eaten – but is used to flavor candy, prepared foods, and is a universal ingredient in cologne.

There really is a Santa Clause – and his bones are in the port city of Bari, Italy, not the North Pole. Present-day Santa is a collection of features from Norse gods, early Christmas poems and cartoons, and various artistic renderings through many generations. But the real Santa can be traced back to 4th-century Christianity and the Greek Bishop Nikolas of Myra, known now as Saint Nicholas, patron saint of sailors and pawnbrokers. Pawnbrokers? Yes, centuries ago, friars ran pawn shops as charities to help the poor, much like today's urban food banks. They provided low-interest loans to poor families, ensuring there was enough food on their tables. Started by the Franciscans, who opened more than 150 of them, *montes pietatius* became widespread throughout Europe. In 1514, even Pope Julius II gave an edict endorsing these institutions, which had become the lifeblood of poor European peasants.

Today, in the fourth year of college, 60% of what students learned in their freshman year is either inaccurate or no longer applies.

Lea & Perrin's sauce is aged for 2 years. This famous Worchestershire sauce was invented by two chemists in England more than 180 years ago. Their first batch was so terrible as to be inedible, so they stored a barrel of it and left it for almost two years. After that time, they decided to taste it one more time before disposing of it forever. The concoction had fermented by that time and they discovered that it was pungent but delicious. Today, the sauce is still fermented for 18 months and is an essential enhancement to many dishes including steak, Caesar's salad and the drink, Bloody Mary. The recipe is a well-kept secret, but one of the ingredients is anchovy.

Tia Zolin Placenta, a hair conditioner used in many salons, is said to come from human placentas.

J. Robert Oppenheimer, "Father" of the atomic bomb, was once considered a national security risk and stripped of all his power.

"Somewhere, something incredible is waiting to be known."

- Carl Sagan.

"Damnation to the beasts" was a capital punishment issued during the Ancient Roman period. It meant execution by lions or other wild beasts.

The first nuclear test bomb was called "Gadget".

The acid in your stomach is strong enough to dissolve razorblades. The reason it doesn't eat away at your stomach is that the cells of your stomach wall renew themselves so frequently that you get a new stomach lining every four days.

Leonardo da Vinci wrote most of his personal notes in cryptic mirror text. The notes on his famous Vitruvian man are in mirror writing. This drawing of a man, (some say a self-portrait) with arms and legs outstretched within a square and circle, actually shows 16 different positions displaying mathematical proportions of the human body. Leonardo never intended this drawing for public display. It was discovered tucked away in a personal notebook. He only used standard writing if he intended his texts to be read by others. The purpose of his practice of mirror writing remains unknown, though several possible reasons have been suggested. For example, writing left handed from left to right would have been messy because the ink just put down would smear as his hand moved across it. Writing in reverse would prevent such smudging. Research suggests that the ability to do mirror writing is probably inherited and caused by atypical language organization in the brain.

The rules of how to pronounce English vowel combinations and the exceptions to those rules makes the process of reading look like learning a complex secret code. Take this sentence for example, "I hear that an early breakfast of peaches, pears and steak is good for your heart". The vowel combination of "ea" is pronounced seven different ways! Think of that the next time you pick up a book or newspaper and glory in the magnificence of your brain. (Now, how does one pronounce "sigh"?)

"...life is tolerable only by the degree of mystification we endow it with."

- E. M. Cioran, *A Short History of Decay*

Fruit flies do not eat the fruit but feed on the yeast that grows as the fruit ages

A giant squid bigger than a school bus washed ashore in New Zealand in 1887. It was more than 55' long! Its eyes were the size of beach balls.

There should be a law that assures the American citizen that the water that comes from our faucets is clean enough to drink. Oh, wait. There is – The EPA's Safe Drinking Water Act passed by congress almost forty years ago. And it's been improved (read "amended") twice since then. Whew! So we're safe, right? Wrong! Each year there are more than 200,000 violations to the Safe Drinking Water Act, and over 20% of those involve city water treatment facilities. Ever wonder what becomes of all the old pills and other medicines people just flush down the toilet. The side effects of these medications are scary, many are even lethal. But even with its amendments, the Safe Drinking Water Act doesn't even allude to the testing for these thousands of contaminates.

At least 100,000 different chemical reactions occur in the normal human brain every second.

"No one can stand in these solitudes unmoved, and not feel that there is more in man than the mere breath of his body."

- Charles Darwin, *The Voyage of the Beagle*

The USS Oriskany is an Essex-class aircraft carrier that was sunk in 2006 to make an artificial reef off the Florida coast. (No passengers were injured in this project.)

Flatworms can learn through ingestion. Certain species of planarians (a type of flatworm) have been gradually taught to run a maze. If you grind them up and feed them to a second batch of planarians, the second batch can run the maze on the first try. (Are cannibals converted as they digest the missionary?)

When he was twelve years old, Paul Tibbets flew in a plane where he dropped candy bars with tiny parachutes onto the people below. Later on, it was the same Paul Tibbets (now a General) tossing out the first atomic bomb on the people of Hiroshima. He named his plane the "Enola Gay" after his mother. Paul had originally studied to become an abdominal surgeon, but dropped out of medical school early because he couldn't stand the sight of blood.

Worldwide, more people die by suicide than by murder.

All varieties of octopuses are venomous. Fortunately, only a few species have enough venom to injure or kill a human being. Octopi inject their venom using a tough beak-like mouth that sticks out of the side of their head. It's similar to a bird's beak and is made of the same tough material as a lobster's shell. Its venom is 10,000 times more powerful than cyanide and the creature can eject the venom into the surrounding water.

> "Her searches after knowledge were arbitrary and without context. It was as if she were shining a small flashlight of curiosity into the dark room of the world."
>
> - Gloria Steinem, *Marilyn*

Anthophobics have an abnormal fear of flowers.

Advertisers of watches understand your subconscious. In almost all commercial and print advertisements, watches and clocks read 10:10. If it's a watch commercial, this is because the hands don't block the brand name. If the time is featured in a commercial or ad for any other product, the hands resemble a person's arms raised in happiness. It is a more positive hand position than the inversion of 8:20, and banks on the theory that a person in a happier frame of mind is easier to persuade.

Rancher Fiona Boyd was leading a stray calf into a shed when the calf's enraged mother suddenly charged her, knocked her down and proceeded to stampede over her. "I was absolutely terrified, and remember rolling up into a ball to protect my head from her hooves," she recalled. That's when my horse, Kerry, who was grazing nearby, immediately leapt to assist her. Her horse bucked and kicked at the cow until it moved away, likely saving Boyd from being trampled to death.

There are more than one million alligators in the state of Florida. Alligators regularly eat pets and farm animals and even people. But, if you're a Bible reader, this may give you some additional hope: In 1971, a farmer on his way home from a local prayer meeting, took a shortcut through a swampy area. He was attacked by an alligator (the man said he thought it was the devil) which bit and locked onto his right thigh. He was able to escape the death trap by beating the "devil" on the head with his bible until the animal finally let go. He made an uncomplicated recovery and now has a new "God-saved-me" story to share with his fellow parishioners.

"The meeting of two personalities is like the contact of two chemical substances. If there is a reaction, both are transformed."

- Carl Jung

Sea otters hold hands when they sleep to keep from drifting apart.

Squirrels plant thousands of new trees each year simply by forgetting where they put their acorns.

Some monkeys in Japan have learned to use coins to buy vending machine snacks.

The # sign is called an octothorpe. In North America it is called a pound sign, whereas everywhere else it's called a hash – the telephone key is called the "hash key"...in blogging it's called hashtag.

> "It is always an attractive moment when curiosity takes hold."
>
> - Damon Galgut

Some states within the US outlaw the collection of rainwater, even on your own property, but allow the sale of barrels and hoses specific to catching and storing that rainwater.

When playing with female puppies, male puppies will often let them win, even if they have a physical advantage.

The queen termite can live up to 50 years and have 30 thousand children per day. A typical colony can contain several egg-laying queens.

It's not just movie hype - a karate chop to the neck can easily interrupt parts of the body, and can also be lethal. Right behind the head at the base of the skull is where the tip of the spine is. Sever or break this and it is all over.

Chimpanzees are great laughers, though they do it differently, on the inhale rather than on the exhale, as we do.

> "...the magical, terrifying and ecstatic realty in which we all live."
>
> - C. S. Lewis

Even blind, deaf, and dumb children laugh naturally.

Some female fireflies, larger than the others (known as femmes fatales) lure their neighbor's mate by mimicking their coded flickering of chemical green light. The males, tricked by the come-hither call, fly to them only to be eaten. in this way, the female acquires a "cannibalistic" tonic that wards off hungry birds and spiders.

Adolf Hitler, Benito Mussolini, and Joseph Stalin were all nominated for the Nobel Peace Prize! Amazingly, the person probably most likely to have deserved the Nobel Peace Prize was never awarded one. Mohandas "Mahatma" Gandhi, Indian leader who advocated non-violence in the struggle for Indian independence from colonial rule, never won the award. He was nominated five times, but failed each time. He was assassinated just two days before the nominations for the 1948 prize were due, which, since he was deceased, disqualified him from the nomination and, therefore, the prize.

Roughly 526,000 people are killed by armed violence each year, making man the second most dangerous animal to man. First, the most dangerous – the mosquito with 725,000 deaths per year. Third place goes to the hippo with 500+ and then lions with a mere 100.

Military snipers are taught to aim at the teeth of the target, because right behind this is the tip of the spine - instant death.

The Catholic Church once banned the use of eyeglasses because it implied that God did not create the human body perfectly.

Edgar Allen Poe and Timothy Leary were cadets at WestPoint Academy. (Imagine if they were bunkmates at the same time.)

Many plants have more genes than humans have.

"Curiosity is the wick in the candle of learning."

- William Arthur Ward

A baby giraffe continues to get its fluid nourishment from the milk of its mother for one year.

Benjamin Franklin invented bifocal spectacles.

In 1999 Brazil issued a set of four stamps smelling of burnt wood to remind people of the danger of careless forest fires....later, they came out with a more esthetic stamp imbued with the aroma of coffee.

Al Capone's brother was a federal prohibition agent.

Coke produces Hi-C Orange, Hi-C Lemonade, Hi-C Punch, and grape soda – no fruit juice in any of them.

The Russian cosmonaut Valeri Polyakov holds the record for the longest time in space – 14 months. One of the most difficult things cosmonauts and astronauts have to get used to upon return to Earth is that things have gravity. They're surprised when they let go of a glass that it falls to the ground.

"There is pleasure in the pathless woods, there is rapture in the lonely shore, there is society where none intrudes, by the deep sea, and music in its roar; I love not Man the less, but Nature more."

- Lord Byron

Parrots blush.

Eugene O'Neil wrote a hit Broadway play that lasted 5 hours.

Benjamin Franklin experimented with leyden jars' electrical charges and once electrocuted a chicken. He was surprised to find the meat tasted uncommonly tender. He speculated it was because the electricity separated the muscle tissues, but in fact it was because the electricity relaxes the muscles and slows rigormortis, which is why poultry farmers still shock birds today before slaughtering them for the grocery store. Franklin even tried the same electrical experiment again, killing the chicken, but then he blew into its lungs and revived it. It jumped up, squawked, and ran into a wall. The electricity had blinded it, but Franklin was the first to use mouth-to-mouth resuscitation to bring a chicken back to life.

Abe Lincoln's mother died when the family dairy cow ate poisonous mushrooms and Ms. Lincoln drank the milk.

Marshmallows are 50% air.

> "For many people who are so lost in their minds, so much involved in their thought processes, the only moments they have when they are not trapped in that are when they are relating to their animal, their pet."
>
> - Eckhart Tolle

The dog evolved from the gray wolf into more than 400 distinct breeds.

The most well-known defensive trait of the common North American opossum is its overwhelming instinct to simply fake death when confronted with danger. This "playing possum" is called thanatosis or tonic immobility and occurs in a surprisingly wide range of animals, from sharks to spiders. But the opossum has another trick up there self-preservation sleeve – they carry a protective protein called LTNF (Lethal Toxin-Neutralizing Factor) that all but makes them immune to the venom of snakes, bees, and scorpions. Once venom is detected within the opossum's body by the protein, it actively seeks it out and sets to work neutralizing it. Amazingly, the marsupial is not only granted immunity to local snakes, but also to snakes on other continents with which it has never had contact. The LTNF protein has been injected into rats, and has apparently been successful in also granting these rodents immunity to otherwise lethal venoms.

Sophomania - the delusion that he or she is of exceptional intelligence.

The hippopotamus is known as one of the deadliest creatures in Africa, responsible for more human fatalities than lions. With razor-sharp teeth and powerful jaws, they can chomp a 10-foot crocodile in half. They can easily outrun humans and reach speeds in excess of 30 miles per hour.

Breakthrough research has actually shown that refined sugar may be more addictive than cocaine!

"The sea was our main entertainment. When company came, we set them before it on rugs, with thermoses and sandwiches and colored umbrellas, as if the water - blue, green, gray, navy or silver as it might be - were enough to watch."

- Sylvia Plath

There are 72 new footballs made exclusively for use in the Super Bowl each year.

John Heiskell, editor of the Arkansas Gazette, covered stories from the first sustained flight of the airplane by the Wright Brothers, the sinking of the Titanic, WWI, the Great Depression, WWII, the Korean War, desegregation, the Vietnam War, and finally, to the Apollo moon landing.

A single teaspoonful of seawater contains about 5 million living creatures.

The USS Abraham Lincoln nuclear powered aircraft carrier has a crew of 5500. For recreation, they formed 22 basketball teams.

John Wilkes Boothe shot Lincoln in a theater and ran to a barn. Lee Harvey Oswald shot Kennedy from a book barn and ran to a theater. Did you know that if Lee Harvey Oswald had not been shot prior to being tired in a court of law, he would have been convicted for killing Officer Tippet? Yep, not many people know anything about Officer Tippet. While fleeing from the Texas Book Depository Building, Oswald was spotted by a cop that had just heard about the assassin's description. When he came after Oswald, Oswald shot him with a pistol and left him for dead. Oswald's initial arrest was for Tippet's murder, not Kennedy's.

"Look at everything always as though you were seeing it either for the first or last time: Thus is your time on earth filled with glory."

- Betty Smith

Polar bears can smell a seal (or a human) from 20 miles away.

Lincoln Logs were invented by Frank Lloyd Wright's son.

Alaska is a land of almost unimaginable scale. Stretching across 586,000 square miles of untamed wilderness, Alaska is one-fifth the size of the contiguous United States. It contains the tallest mountain in North America, Mt. McKinley, which many Alaskans simply call "the mountain." And of course, the Land of the Midnight Sun has longer summer days than any other state. This majestic landscape borders two oceans and three seas, with a 47,300 mile coastline. Alaska boasts over three million lakes, 3,000 rivers, 1,800 islands, and more than 100,000 glaciers.

The number one cause of blindness in adults in the United States is diabetes.

"What a marvel of design is the human hand. The hand is action, it digs roads and builds cities, it throws spears and diapers babies. And even a small drama like pushing a button can change the course of nations. Nerves in our hands send messages about touch, pressure, heat, cold, and pain up 17,000 fibers to the brain. Without that intricate feel for life there would be no artists to make sensory and emotional maps of the world. We've become voluptuaries of touch. We feel our way through life from birth to death. After all, touch is what leads us outside ourselves. Touch is what gives us our grasp on life. But most of all it allows us to rejoice in one another, our friends and loved ones, our neighbors and families. And perhaps that is the most touching thought of all."

– Diane Ackerman, *Deep Play*

Al'Khwarizmi, who lived in Baghdad around the year 800 A.D., calculated a more precise value of 3.1416 for pi – the ratio of athe radius of a circle to its circumference. This is a computational feat equal only to modern computers. His name lives on in the term "algorithm." The title of one of his books, "al-Jabr", which means "completion" or "restoration" gave us the word "algebra."

While our forefathers were trying to negotiate with King George III regarding their discontent with England's harsh taxation policies, George Washington had already decided that combat and bloodshed were already a predetermined fix. He even made his will conspicuous by showing up to the Continental Congress in full dress military uniform. Many historians believe that it was Washington's strong-jawed intention that singularly obliged the American Revolution.

Every continent begins and ends in the same letter. e.g. AfricA, EuropE, AsiA, AustraliA, AntarcticA.

The largest earthworm on record was found in South Africa and measured 22 feet. (The early bird catches the worm...or vice versa.)

Pussums cannot hang by their tail. But when they play dead, they emit a foul smell and froth at the mouth to add to their disguise.

"The perfect stillness of the night was thrilled by a more solemn silence. The darkness held a presence that was all the more felt because it was not seen. I could not anymore have doubted that He was there than I was. Indeed, I felt myself to be, if possible, the less real of the two."

– William James, *The Varieties of Religious Experience*

Ironically, watermelons, which are 92% water, originated from the Kalahari Desert in Africa.

The National Geographic magazine is published in 38 different languages.

Percentage of Africa that is wilderness: 28%. Percentage of North America that is wilderness: 38%.

Alexander Graham Bell was the second President of the National Geographic magazine.

For more than 3,000 years, Carpenter ants have been used to close wounds in India, Asia and South America.

"Standing on a hill in the East African plains, I saw herds of thousands of wild beasts, grazing in soundless peace, beneath the primeval world, as they had done for unimaginable ages of time. And I had the feeling of being the first man, to first being to know all this. The whole world around me was still in the primitive silence and knew not that it was. In this very moment in which I knew it, the world came into existence, and without this moment it would never have been."

– Carl Jung

Ninety-five percent of tropical fish sold in North America originate from Florida.

Any animal that has skin hair or fur can get dandruff, but in animals it is called "dander".

Lee Harvey Oswald, the infamous assassin of President John F. Kennedy, was a former marine who defected to Russia, but after not too long there, he begged to return.

It is impossible to find the circumference of a circle without knowing the true value of pi (the ratio of a circle's circumference to its diameter).

skanagoah – the Lakota Indian word for "the still, electrifying awareness one experiences in the deep woods"

– Pam Colorado, *New Voices from the Longhouse*

The book <u>Ulysses</u> by the Irish author James Joyce, was so controversial that it was deemed dangerous and banned by entire governments. In a famous 1933 court decision, Judge John M. Woolsey declared it an emetic book – emetic means "causing one to vomit". (Makes you want to grab a copy and read it right away, yes? But be warned, while it might not induce nausea, it does contains a single sentence of 4,391 words!)

Tiny windows in a bird's wing open and close as it flaps, letting air through only on the upstroke.

For the blockbuster movie "The Terminator," O.J. Simpson was considered to play the role of the Terminator, but producers did not choose him as they thought he would not be taken seriously.

> "Being at ease with not knowing is crucial for answers to come to you."
>
> - Eckhart Tolle

The reason the Animal Crackers box is designed with a string handle is because when the popular circus theme was introduced in 1902 they thought it would also be a good idea to package them with a string as a Christmas novelty so they could be hung from Christmas trees.

Scientists recently found the fossils of an ancestor of the cockroach that was 7 feet long.

A bomb dropped by the Allies on Berlin during World War II killed every animal in the Berlin Zoo except the elephant, which escaped and roamed the city. When a Russian commander saw hungry Germans chasing the elephant and trying to kill it, he ordered his troops to protect it and shoot anyone who tried to kill it.

Humans have about 10 thousand taste buds. Catfish have about 250 thousand. Chickens have about 2 dozen. (But which one tastes better?)

The word "limelight", is commonly used today to refer to lead performances in theatre. It originated before electricity when lime was burned in a lamp, which created a white light that was directed at the performers.

Trypophobics have an irrational and persistent fear of holes.

The largest coral reef in the world is the Great Barrier Reef located in Australia. The reef is approximately 2023 kilometers long – that's almost halfway across the United States.

Chickens are smarter than dogs.

Paul Johnson and Paul Kenny of Scripps Research Center performed a study which concluded that junk food has similar addictive qualities as that of heroin. McDonalds calls frequent buyers of their food "heavy users".

"Wealth is the ability to fully experience life."

- Henry David Thoreau

Twice as tall as the Statue of Liberty, "Zumanjaro: Drop of Doom" at the Six Flags adventure park in Jackson, New Jersey, reaches speeds of over 90 miles an hour in a ten second free fall. Standing at 414 feet, it allows riders to catch sight of Philadelphia's skyscrapers, more than 50 miles away.

Penguins have one mate for life. They "sing" to each other to learn and recognize each others' voices.

"The most beautiful experience we can have is the mysterious. It is the fundamental emotion which stands at the cradle of true art and true science."

- Albert Einstein, *The World As I See It*

We spray our countertops and grimace when someone sneezes near us—in fact, we do everything we can to avoid unnecessary encounters with the germ world. But the truth is we are practically walking condos rife with bacterial colonies from our skin to the deepest recesses of our guts. Microbiologists estimate that bacterial cells outnumber our human cells 10 to one, leading one scientist to state, "We are in essence only ten percent human - the rest is pure microbe". There are about 500 different species of bacteria on and in your body. We've evolved a symbiotic relationship with them. In return for food and board, bacteria help us with digestion, vitamin production and keeping our immune system strong. Without them, you'd probably never see your next birthday. Our relationship with the 100 trillion single-celled friends is so strong that some scientist have come to regard us and our hitchhikers as one human-bacteria super-organism – or, put another way, Dr. Roy Slater, who has studied the subject for more than four years, says, "Bacteria have now come to be regarded as a virtual organ with the combined output far in excess of the liver".

"Why are we reading, if not in hope of beauty laid bare, life heightened and its deepest mystery probed? Can the writer isolate and vivify all in experience that most deeply engages our intellects and our hearts? Can the writer renew our hope for literary forms? Why are we reading if not in hope that the writer will magnify and dramatize our days, will illuminate and inspire us with wisdom, courage, and the possibility of meaningfulness, and will press upon our minds the deepest mysteries, so that we may feel again their majesty and power? What do we ever know that is higher than that power which, from time to time, seizes our lives, and reveals us startlingly to ourselves as creatures set down here bewildered? Why does death so catch us by surprise, and why love? We still and always want waking."

- Annie Dillard

52788145R00066

Made in the USA
Middletown, DE
22 November 2017